• LEARNING HOW •
Skateboarding

BY
JANE MERSKY LEDER

Bancroft-Sage Publishing
601 Elkcam Circle, Suite C-7, P. O. 355   Marco, Florida 33969-0355 USA

• LEARNING HOW •
Skateboarding

AUTHOR
JANE MERSKY LEDER

EDITED BY
JODY JAMES

DESIGNED BY
CONCEPT and DESIGN

PHOTO CREDITS

Alan Leder: Cover, Pages 4, 6, 7, 9, 10, 11, 12, 13, 14, 15, 16, 17, 19, 20, 21, 22, 23, 24, 27, 30, 31, 32, 36, 37.
Unicorn Stock Photos:
Aneal Vohra - Pages 5, 44;
Steve Bourgeois - Page 43.
Richard Noll: Pages 29, 33, 34, 38, 41, 42.
J. Grant Brittian: Pages 25, 35, 48.

ACKNOWLEDGMENTS

Alan and I would like to thank the Bosworth Street skateboarders: Anton, Devin, Johanes, and Aja. You were all terrific! And many thanks to Dan Field, owner of Sessions Skateboard Shop in Chicago, Illinois, and his trusty salesperson and skateboard enthusiast Boyd Bruner. Without their help, this book could never have been produced. Finally, hats off to Don Bostick, the President of the National Skateboard Association, for taking the time to go over a copy of the book with an expert's eye and to coach me through some of skateboarding's more difficult moves and concepts.

TABLE OF CONTENTS

**LIBRARY OF CONGRESS
CATALOGING-IN-PUBLICATION DATA**

Leder, Jane Mersky.
    Learning how: skateboarding / by Jane Mersky Leder; edited by Jody James;
illustrated by Concept and Design.
        p.   cm. – (Learning how sports)
    Summary: Examines the history, equipment, rules, contests, and prominent perform-
ers of skateboarding.
    ISBN 0-944280-33-1 (lib. bdg.) – ISBN 0-944280-42-0 (pbk.)
    1. Skateboarding – Juvenile literature. [1. Skateboarding.]   I. Title.   II. Title:
Skateboarding.   III. Series.
    GV859.8.L43   1991
    796.2'1–dc20   91-23530
                                                            CIP
                                                            AC

**International Standard
Book Number:**
Library Binding 0-944280-33-1
Paperback Binding 0-944280-42-0

**Library of Congress
Catalog Card Number:**
91-23530

INTRODUCTION

This is a big day for the kids who live on Bosworth Street. They have waited a long time to skateboard together. They saved their money to buy the equipment they needed. They talked to the owner of the local skateboard store about the best way to learn how to skateboard. Then they went to the library and read about skateboarding.

Learning how to skateboard can be fun!

They discovered that skateboarding is not a new sport. It began in California in the 1960s and was sometimes called "sidewalk surfing." Some people saw skateboarding as surfing without water.

In the mid-1970s, skateboard companies designed new, bigger skateboards that were easier to ride. The companies also introduced plastic wheels. The plastic wheels allow skaters to ride their skateboards on many kinds of surfaces.

Skateboarding has become very popular among young people. It is estimated that there are now as many as 20 million skateboarders in the United States.

Skateboarding began in California in the 1960s and was sometimes called, "Sidewalk Surfing."

CHAPTER ONE:

The Parts of a Skateboard

Every part of a skateboard has a job to do. The parts all work together to make the skateboard work properly and safely. Therefore, it is important to know the different parts of a skateboard and what each part does.

The Deck

Most skaters refer to the top of the skateboard as the **deck** or *board*. In some areas, people also call it a *stick*, a *blank*, a *top*, or an *axe*. Most decks are made of several layers of wood that are pressed together with a polyvinyl glue. This combination of wood and glue is placed into a

The most common name for the top of your skateboard is the deck or board.

6

specially shaped mold and pressure is applied. After the mixture hardens, the mold is removed. This specially shaped piece is now called a deck *blank*.

The blank is then formed into one of the various shapes and sizes of a skateboard. Some skateboard manufacturers place a thin fiberglass skin over the top layer of the shaped deck wood. This skin makes the deck stronger and more flexible. There are several types of skateboard decks. These decks come in many different shapes. The shape refers to the outline of the deck, which includes the *nose* (front), *tail* (back), and *rails* (sides).

There are many different sizes and shapes of skateboards.

The basic skateboard deck has rails that curve upward and a nose that is "kicked" upward. The deck flattens slightly in the middle and then curves upward, forming the kicktail. This shape allows your feet to grip the deck better and gives you more control when you skateboard.

A **vert deck** is larger than most boards. It is mainly for vertical ramp riding, and is used by the more advanced skaters.

Street or **mini decks** are used on the street. They are smaller versions of the larger vert decks. These decks are usually around 9 1/2 inches wide by 29 1/2 inches long.

Freestyle decks are the smallest decks (usually 7 1/2 inches by 28 inches). They are rectangular in shape. This design makes the skateboard more suitable for **freestyle** skateboarding. Fast footwork, spins, and flips are easier to do with a freestyle deck.

Longboards, as you can guess, are longer than other skateboards. They are usually 36 inches to 40 inches long and 10 inches wide. Longboards give you a "surfing" type of feel when you ride them.

Which type of deck should you choose? Remember that the size of a skateboard deck must match the size of the skater. If you are 5'6" or taller, you can choose from all deck sizes, but a vert or large deck is best. If you are under 5'6", you should probably choose a street or mini deck.

The Wheels

Every skateboard requires two sets of wheels. The wheels are made of a flexible plastic called **urethane**. Even though they are all made of urethane, skateboard wheels differ in many ways. Some wheels are hard and others are soft. The word **durometer** refers to the hardness of the wheels.

Most beginners should start with wheels that have a softer durometer. These wheels do not catch on rocks, glass, or cracks as easily as the harder wheels. Softer wheels also grip the riding surface better.

Wheels also have different widths. A wider wheel starts more slowly and is slightly heavier. It is designed for high speed and skating on uneven surfaces. A narrow wheel starts more quickly but has a slower top speed.

Wheels also come in many different colors. A common myth is that some colors of urethane wheels are faster than others. The truth is that all the colors have more or less the same speed.

Skateboard wheels come in many colors. Some wheels are harder than others, and some wheels are wider than others. Each is designed for a specific purpose.

The Truck

The aluminum wheel assemblies that allow the skateboard to turn are called **trucks**. There are two trucks on every skateboard. The wheels are attached to the trucks. *Bearings* inside the trucks allow the skateboard wheels to turn in the direction the rider leans. Most of the better trucks are made from aircraft grade aluminum that is polished, painted, and hardened for strength.

The wheel assemblies that allow the skateboard to turn are called trucks. There are two trucks on every skateboard.

Putting the Skateboard Together

Many beginners prefer to buy a skateboard that has already been put together. Others buy the parts and have someone at their local skateboard store assemble the skateboard.

To assemble a skateboard, you must first "tape" the skateboard deck. Cut a piece of rough, sandpaperlike material called **griptape** the size of the skateboard deck. Then shape the griptape to fit the skateboard exactly. Griptape is a must for safety because it helps a skater's feet stay on the board.

Next, attach the nose, tail, and rail guards to the deck. These plastic guards protect the front, back, and sides of the deck from impact and wear. After the plastic guards are in place, attach the trucks that connect the wheels to the deck. Then attach the wheels to the trucks.

Putting together a skateboard may be something that you never will need to do. However, you should get to know your board. You should give it a safety check each time before you ride. Check for damage to your board, trucks, and wheels. Make sure that all the nuts and screws are tight.

Griptape must be applied to the skateboard deck. This is a must for safety because it helps a skater's feet stay on the board.

CHAPTER TWO:

Safety Gear

Every skater should wear safety gear. Wearing safety gear is the only way to limit the chance of injury. A complete set of safety gear includes a **helmet**, **wrist guards**, **gloves**, **kneepads**, and **elbow pads**.

A complete set of safety gear can be expensive. If you cannot afford to buy it all, you should talk to someone who works in a local skateboard store. The owner or salesperson can suggest the gear that is most important for the kind of skating you plan to do.

Every skater should wear safety gear. A helmet is very important.

Wristguards, elbow pads, kneepads and gloves are all part of the safety gear worn by skateboarders.

There is always a risk of falling and hitting your head when you are skateboarding, particularly if you are going very fast or riding on a vertical ramp. A helmet will protect your head from serious injury.

Wrist guards protect your wrists and hands from injury when you fall hands-first. Most people put their hands down to break the impact when they fall. Gloves are also good for protection against palm bruises and scrapes that you may get when you fall.

Kneepads are pads that have plastic cups to help protect your knees. Elbow pads are built in the same way as kneepads. They protect your elbows from scrapes and sometimes even from breaks.

A helmet will protect your head from injury during a fall.

Plastic cups help protect your knees from injury.

The kids from Bosworth Street are ready to ride—almost. First, they all need to put on their safety gear. They also need to check their skateboards to make sure that there is no damage and that all the nuts and screws are tight.

Before starting to ride, check your skateboard to make sure all nuts and screws are tight.

There is plenty of talk about where to ride. They decide to stay in the neighborhood. They will practice on the sidewalk in front of their homes. A grassy area runs between the sidewalk and Bosworth Street. The grass makes riding on the sidewalk there safer.

The kids know it is important to clean the sidewalk before they start. They take turns sweeping the leaves and looking for glass, rocks, or anything else that could be dangerous to skate over.

Make sure the sidewalk or riding surface is swept clean of all debris.

CHAPTER THREE:

The ABCs of Skateboarding

The basic idea of learning to do anything on a skateboard is to work up to it slowly. It is best to get the "feel" of the board before you start moving. Put the board on a flat surface so that it will not move. That makes it easier to stand and balance without worrying about falling.

Standing on the Skateboard

When you stand on the skateboard, do what is natural for you. If you put your left foot forward and your right foot back, you are in what is called the **regular stance**. If you ride with your right foot forward and your left foot back, you are riding **goofy foot**. It does not matter which foot you put forward. What is important is that it feels comfortable and natural to you.

While you are standing still, you might tip the skateboard from side to side. Bend your knees a little. That will help you tip the board without falling off. Bend over and look at the wheels as you tip the skateboard. See how they steer? That is how a skateboard works. If you tip to the right, the wheels steer to the right. If you tip to the left, the wheels steer to the left.

If you put your left foot forward and your right foot back, you are in a "regular stance".

To steer your skateboard, you must tip it slightly from side to side. If you tip to the right, the wheels steer to the right. If you tip to the left, the wheels steer to the left.

Time to Start Moving

The time has come to start moving on your skateboard. Stand next to the board and put one foot on it. To get moving, give a little push with the foot that is on the ground.

You do not have to put your pushing foot on the skateboard right away. In case you lose your balance, you can just set that foot down to avoid a fall. Once you begin to coast, lift your pushing foot onto the board. Now you are cruising!

To begin moving, put one foot on the skateboard and give a little push with the foot that is on the ground.

You may wobble a lot during your first attempts. Don't worry—your ankles will get stronger and less wobbly with time. Concentrate on keeping your knees bent a little, and try to look forward. That way, your feet will "learn" the feel of the skateboard. The rest of your body will get into the habit of going straight forward.

Some skaters like to put their hands out in front of their bodies a little to steady themselves. If you do this, do not "flap" your elbows all over the place. Just move your hands forward from your waist.

Concentrate on keeping your knees bent a little, and try to look forward.

Stopping

Skateboards do not have brakes. Your feet have to do the stopping for you. For beginners, stopping is a three-step process. First, move your back foot off the board and hold it there for a moment. Then lower that foot to the ground. With the other foot, quickly step off the skateboard ahead of the first foot. Keep running ahead of the skateboard until you can stop.

To stop your skateboard, move your back foot off the board and hold it there for a moment.

Then lower that foot to the ground.

With the other foot, step off the skateboard ahead of the first foot. Keep running ahead of the skateboard until you can stop.

More advanced skaters often do what is called a **wheelie** stop. To do a wheelie, raise the nose wheels high enough to drag the tail of the skateboard on the ground. Dragging the tail slows the board to a stop.

Wheelies stop the skateboard and look professional. But do not try a wheelie until you have a good feel for your skateboard and have learned the more basic stop.

More advanced skaters often do a wheelie.

The best skaters do what is called a **front-side slide** to stop. This stop involves throwing your arms out in front of you and turning the skateboard in the direction you are facing. This movement unweights the board and causes it to slide sideways. By putting even pressure on both your front and back leg, you can control the slide as the board comes to a stop.

The front-side slide is a way to stop, used only by the best skaters.

Turning

Turning is a skill that you have to learn slowly. You need to learn how to control the turns a little bit at a time. Your first turns should be slow and very wide. When you can do the slow turns, you can start making your turns faster and tighter.

For your first turns, try to find a smooth, gradual slope that levels off after a few yards. As you coast slowly down the slope, tip the skateboard very slightly with your feet in the direction you wish to turn. Do not make a sudden, jerking move. Just think, "turn, feet."

You must lean into any turn to keep from falling off the skateboard. If you want to turn to the right, lean to the right just before the skateboard is all the way into the turn. If you want to turn to the left, lean to the left. Lean forward a little, as well. Do not twist your head, shoulders, and hips before the skateboard starts to come around. Twisting your body too soon sets you up for a possible fall.

While you are learning, make sure you finish one turn completely before you start another. The ends of turns can be tricky. There is not much keeping you steady on the skateboard. At first, you will probably wobble after a turn. With practice, your ankles will get stronger, and the wobbling will stop.

Turning is a skill to learn slowly. Your first turns should be slow and very wide.

Learning How to Fall

Everyone falls—even the professionals. It is a good idea to learn how to fall before you go head-on into it. You can practice falling and rolling on grass. That way, you can learn to fall without hurting yourself seriously. If you do it wrong, just try again.

The most important thing is to relax. If you are about to fall, tuck your head down. Drop one shoulder in the direction you are falling. Keep your elbows close to your body. As you hit the ground, keep rolling until your body comes to a natural stop.

Since falling correctly is very important, practice on a soft surface, such as grass, until you can fall properly. Also, wear safety gear and try new tricks on a soft surface before you do them on cement. These practices will cut down the number of injuries you receive when you do fall.

More and more skaters are learning how to do a **knee slide** when they fall. Done properly, a knee slide is actually a safer way to fall because it reduces the impact and is less jolting to the body.

Before you try a knee slide, you must have good kneepads. The plastic cups in the pads should be in top shape. A knee slide is not hard to do. When you are about to fall, you drop down to both knees and slide to a stop.

Skaters who skate ramps should also buy pads called **gaskets**. Gaskets are made out of the same material as wet suits. Put one over each knee under the kneepads. Gaskets help keep the kneepads in place and act as a knee brace. They are essential for stopping on ramps when doing a knee slide.

Anyone can learn to do a knee slide. But, remember: it is crucial that you wear good kneepads. And, if you are skating on ramps, use a gasket on each knee.

This professional skateboarder is doing a "Front-Side Grind". He is also wearing gaskets. Gaskets help keep the kneepads in place and act as a knee brace.

Tips for New Skaters

The kids on Bosworth Street practiced riding, turning, and stopping every day after school. They loved the free feeling they got as they coasted down the sidewalk. Sure, they took falls every now and then. But the falls were part of the sport.

Practicing every day will make you a good skateboarder.

One warm, cloudy Saturday afternoon, the kids decided to walk to the cement boardwalk along Lake Michigan. They had heard that this was a great place to skateboard. No cars were allowed and there were very few pedestrians. There was even a ramp where brave skaters could practice tricks.

As they walked along the boardwalk, the kids talked about some of the tips the owner of the local skateboard store had given them.

"Take it slow," he had said, "and don't skate beyond your ability. And *always* wear your safety gear." The kids from Bosworth Street took his advice seriously.

The kids also remembered him saying that skateboards get stolen very easily. They each vowed to watch their skateboards or to keep the skateboards under their feet.

They also discussed how water, more than anything else, can damage a skateboard. It was a cloudy day, but there was no rain. If it started to rain, the kids decided, they would head for home right away. They did not want to take the chance of damaging their skateboards.

The kids talked about the tips they had gotten from their local skateboard store - "take it slow and don't skate beyond your ability."

CHAPTER FOUR:

Basic Tricks

Once you learn how to push off, turn, and stop, you may want to learn some basic tricks. The key is to take your time and to be patient and always wear safety gear. You can expect to take your share of falls each time you begin to learn a new trick.

After you begin to feel comfortable with your skateboard, you may want to learn some basic tricks.

Many skaters want to do an **ollie**. The best way to describe an ollie is jumping up in the air with the skateboard. When an ollie is done well, the skater is suspended in the air with the skateboard underfoot. A well-done ollie makes you wonder whether the skateboard is glued to the skater's feet. (Of course, it is not.)

To do an ollie, you push your feet down as hard as you can on the tail of the skateboard. You can hear the tail hit the ground. When it hits, you push your front foot forward, which brings the tail off the ground.

An "Ollie" is a trick performed by the advanced skateboarder.

There are many different kinds of ollies. For now, you might be interested in knowing that an *ollie 180* is a move where the skater turns a half circle in the air. If the skater turns toward the front, it is called a *front-side 180*. If he turns toward the back, it is called *back-side 180*.

Professional skateboarder, Tony Hawk does a "One-Footed Fakie Ollie".

A **grind** is another trick that skaters enjoy. The skater grinds the trucks of the skateboard on a curb, a **railslide bar**, or the **metal coping** at the top of a ramp. When a skater does a grind, his trucks make a loud noise. Most skateboard videos show a skater doing a grind. It is not only a loud trick, but also an impressive one.

It should come as no surprise that there are many different kinds of grinds. A skater can do a *front-side, backside, 50/50, Smith*, or *feeble grind*. The best way to understand the difference between the grinds is to either watch a skateboard video or talk to an advanced skater.

This skater is performing a trick called a front-side grind on a mini ramp.

Each of the kids from Bosworth Street took advantage of the wide boardwalk to practice basic skills and try new tricks. It was fun to practice big turns in such a large area. It felt good to push off and coast for what seemed like forever. And there was plenty of room to practice wheelies.

Devin perfected a trick called **walking the board**. He stood with both feet near the back of the board. When he was balanced on the skateboard, he took two quick little steps toward the nose of the board. As he got better, he made it look like he was flicking the board forward and back without any effort.

"Walking the Board" can be a lot of fun.

Anton tried to do a **rock and roll boardslide**. That is a skateboarding move where the skateboard slides along on a curb or along the **lip** of a ramp. It is not such an easy trick to do. He almost fell several times.

After an afternoon of skating, the kids from Bosworth Street were tired. But skateboarding had been fun. They had discovered a world of escape and freedom that all of them enjoyed. As they relaxed after a "hard" day, they talked about going to a skatepark to watch more advanced skaters. There they could see some of the best skaters doing incredible tricks.

Skateboarding can give you a feeling of accomplishment and freedom.

Skateparks

A **skatepark** is an indoor or outdoor facility where skaters can use ramps and obstacles to practice their skating. Skateparks provide a safe environment that is free of cars and pedestrians. For these reasons, many skateboard contests take place at skateparks. Some skateparks even rent safety gear. Many of them also have pro shops where skaters can buy the newest equipment and talk to experts.

Most skateparks have two basic kinds of ramps, **mini ramps** and **vert ramps**. Because there is no one set of rules, the size and shape of these ramps keep changing.

The important difference between vert ramps and mini ramps is that vert ramps "go to vertical," and mini ramps do not. *Vertical* means "straight up and down." All vert ramps have at least one, and usually two, walls that are vertical.

One of the basic ramps found at a skate park is the vert ramp - its walls are vertical.

Many vert ramps are shaped like a *U*. The *arc* or *transition* (the curved area) often measures between 9 and 9 1/2 feet. The vertical section is at the top of the ramp. It often measures 1 1/2 feet. That makes a vert ramp between 10 1/2 and 11 feet high.

There is a metal lip at the top of each side of a vert ramp. Skaters often like to grind their trucks on it when they reach the top.

Vert ramps are made of wood or steel. The steel ramps last longer, but it hurts more when you fall on them. Whether a ramp is made of steel or wood, it is important to wear your safety gear.

Skaters can do all kinds of tricks on a vert ramp. They can leave the ramp, fly up in the air, and come back down. They can do flips in the air. They can do a handstand, balancing the board on their feet. These tricks have funny names like *ollie air, invert, body jar,* and *nollie.*

A ramp that has two sides, or walls, is called a **half-pipe ramp**. Because of their size and structure, half-pipe ramps are usually permanent. They cannot be moved from place to place.

Mini ramps, unlike vert ramps, do not have vertical walls. If a mini has two sides, or walls, it is a half-pipe ramp. If it has only one side, or wall, it is a **quarter-pipe ramp**. Mini ramps are always lower than vert ramps. Again, the sizes keep changing. Today, the average mini ramp is between 4 and 6 1/2 feet high.

Mini ramps are not permanent structures. They can be moved from place to place. Mini ramps can be put together end-to-end, too. Skaters can do tricks over the spine (where the two lips meet) to go from one mini ramp to the other.

Skateparks usually have several different mini ramps that vary in size. Skaters can do a variety of tricks on them. These tricks have unusual names like *nose stall, air-to-fakie, chink-chink*, and *nose blunt.*

In addition to ramps, many skateboard parks have what is called a **street area**. These areas are built to resemble street structures such as curbs, sidewalks, and railslides. Street areas often include quarter-pipe ramps of different sizes, slider bars, simulated parking curbs, and simulated sidewalks.

Contests

Many skaters like to take part in amateur or professional competitions, or contests, sponsored by the National Skateboard Association (NSA). The NSA sets the rules for these contests and tries to make skateboarding a safe sport. The NSA stresses that skaters should always wear the proper safety gear.

The NSA contests are held in cities both in the United States and in Europe. The competitions are open to all professional (pro) skaters.

Professional skaters receive prize money, contracts for product endorsements, and *royalties* for skateboards (and other items) that bear their names. Most pro skaters design the graphics for and the shape of the skateboard that bears their signature. Many of these skaters are available for autograph sessions and demonstrations.

Each pro skater is sponsored by one of the companies that makes skateboarding equipment. The sponsor pays the contest entry fees. Sponsors also pay the entry fees for the top amateur skaters. The amateurs do not earn prize money or money from the sale of skateboarding products. Many amateur skaters hope to become pros. If they win a major NSA contest, chances are good that they will be recognized as professionals.

The National Skateboard Association sponsors both amateur and professional competitions. This skateboarder does a "Front-Side Air".

Skateboarding contests are divided into events, or categories. Some contests have four different events: vert, street, mini, and freestyle. Freestyle skateboarding is much like freestyle ice skating. The skaters use a freestyle skateboard. They do spins, kick flips, and a lot of other fancy footwork. The best freestyle skaters are very graceful. Their performances are like dances.

A new skateboarding event that is becoming more and more popular is called **flatland**. Flatland skating is similar to freestyle skating. The difference is the width of the skateboard that the skaters use. Flatland skateboards are wider. Most of them are at least 8 1/2 inches wide. The flatland event has been created for those skaters who borrow tricks from freestylers and do them on the street.

Tony Hawk, a professional skateboarder, does a "Chink-Chink" on a mini ramp.

Conclusion

The kids on Bosworth Street, like many other young people, are excited about skateboarding. Unlike many other sports, skateboarding allows them to skate when they want and where they want. They do not need a team to skate.

Many young people are excited about skateboarding.

Skateboarding is fast and it is fun. It gives skaters a sense of freedom like a bird soaring through the air. Welcome to the exciting world of skateboarding!

Skateboarding gives you a sense of freedom!

GLOSSARY

deck - the top of the skateboard

durometer [duh *RAHM* eht uhr] - the hardness of a skateboard wheel

elbow pads - pads with plastic cups that protect the skater's elbows

flatland - a type of skateboarding that is similar to freestyle, but is performed on a wider board

freestyle - a type of skateboarding that involves footwork, board spins, and kick flips

freestyle deck - the smallest type of deck used in freestyle skateboarding

front-side slide - a more advanced way of stopping on a skateboard

gasket - a special pad worn under a kneepad that helps keep the kneepad in place when a skater does a knee slide

gloves - safety gear that protects a skater's palms from bruises and scrapes

goofy foot - skateboarding with right foot forward on the deck

grind - a basic trick in which the trucks grind along a curb or the lip of a ramp

griptape [GRIHP tayp] - sandpaperlike material that is taped on the deck to help the skater's feet stay on the deck

half-pipe ramp - a ramp that has two sides

helmet - safety gear that protects the skater's head from serious injury

kneepads - safety gear that protects the skater's knees from serious injury

knee slide - a more advanced way to stop; skater drops down to both knees and slides to a stop

lip - the metal coping along the top of a ramp

longboard - the longest of the skateboard decks

metal coping - a piece of metal piping attached to the top of a skateboard ramp so that skaters can do a grind

mini deck - smaller version of vert deck

mini ramp - smaller version of vert ramp

ollie [*AH* lee] - a basic skateboard trick in which the board is lifted off the ground

quarter pipe ramp - a ramp that has only one side

railslide bar - wood with metal coping used at skateparks to simulate a curb or railing for doing a grind

regular stance - left foot forward when riding a skateboard

rock and roll boardslide - a skate move in which the board slides along its rails on the lip of a ramp or curb

skatepark - an indoor or outdoor facility where skaters can use ramps and obstacles to practice

street area - an area in a skatepark that recreates structures such as curbs, sidewalks, and railslides

truck - the aluminum wheel assembly that makes a skateboard turn

urethane - a flexible plastic from which skateboard wheels are made

vert deck - a large deck that is used for vertical ramps

vert ramp - a ramp that has at least one side that "goes to vertical" (straight up and down)

walking the board - a trick in which a skater starts at the back of the board and takes a series of short steps toward the front

wheelie - a way of stopping a skateboard by raising the front wheels high enough to drag the tail of the skateboard on the ground

wrist guards - safety gear that protects a skater's wrists and hands